SELLING
TO
STRANGERS

The Secrets of How to
Sell to Anybody

Robert D. Gibson

Table of Content

Introduction

People are constantly attempting to influence one another, whether it be in the hallways of their high school or the corridors of power. We make an effort to persuade people to enjoy the books and music we do. We want coworkers to adopt the changes we suggest at work. We advocate for the political parties we support among our friends and family. However, have you ever observed that certain individuals are more adept at persuasion than others? They persuade people to share their opinions and agree with them. These folks are skilled at closing deals, securing political victories, and perhaps even landing dates. Why is this the case? Charming? Allure? Nice appearance?

Through this book, we will learn the specifics of comprehending the thoughts and emotions of people we have never met before. It is a resource for turning onlookers into ardent customers—from reading the veiled intentions of strangers to adjusting to a constantly shifting market.

Every conversation, every sales pitch, and every deal present an opportunity for you to tell a compelling story, form a connection with a customer, and ultimately win over that customer for life. Whether you are an experienced salesperson, an aspiring business owner, or a marketing enthusiast, this book is your ticket to overcoming the difficulties and enjoying the benefits of making sales to strangers. Welcome to the world of selling to strangers.

Chapter 1

The Psychology of Persuasion: Understanding the Strangers' Mind

Every effective sales interaction starts with a deep understanding of human psychology. Like any other person, strangers are impacted by a wide range of conscious and subconscious factors that affect their decisions. Sales professionals can gain insightful knowledge of the minds of strangers by studying the psychology of persuasion. This knowledge enables them to foresee responses, understand motivations, and adjust their strategies accordingly.

Comprehending the Decision-Making Process

When presented with a purchasing decision, strangers go through a convoluted thought process. In this process, needs are assessed, options are considered, risks are considered, and emotional validation is sought. Persuasive salespeople are aware of this order and modify their presentations to fit the strangers' decision-making process. By putting themselves in strangers' shoes with empathy, they can address issues and emphasize advantages in a way that connects.

Fundamental Ideas in Persuasion

Negotiation is the process of persuasion. Nothing is done on its own. You have nothing to work with when trying to persuade someone to support you if you can't offer them something of value. Psychology holds that the best approach to persuading and influencing people is contingent upon several variables, such as the message's nature, the audience, and the communication context. Nonetheless, the following broad guidelines may be useful:

1. WIIFM: Look up those characters online. What's in it for me is what the acronym stands for. In any case, it's a solid beginning. It is a procedure for outlining the reasons why the other person ought to or might lean toward you. You are fighting a losing battle if you do not offer the other person anything of value.

2. Make an effort to touch their charitable side. Most people desire to help others and show them kindness. Offer them the opportunity to assist you or show you kindness if you are speaking with someone similar to that.

3. Make use of reciprocity and guilt's beautiful qualities. When a friend yells, "First round on me!" you might instantly think, "I got the second then!" That's because we're wired to return favors and

it's only just. Hence, consider any "good deed" you perform for someone as an investment in your future. It will inspire people to give back. Influencing people can be accomplished through the use of reciprocity, which is providing something of value before requesting something in return.

4. Commitment and consistency: Individuals are more inclined to act in a way that is in line with their beliefs or past behaviors. Influencing others can be accomplished by being consistent, e.g., by framing your message in a way that aligns with the recipient's preexisting beliefs. We frequently tend to stick to our previous choices and behaviors. This idea can be applied by encouraging people to make modest commitments and then progressively raising them.

5. Make use of social proof: People are more likely to be swayed by the beliefs and actions of people whom they identify as being like them. You can persuade people by using social proof, like case studies or testimonies. This idea can be applied by showcasing a product's popularity or providing proof that others have carried out your request.

6. Liking: We usually accede to requests from people we know well, but why do we accede to requests from total strangers? People who are similar to us are liked by us by nature. In the workplace, this can be used to break the ice and discover common ground such as shared friends, hometowns, sports interests, or schools. To like people and gain their favor, we search for commonalities. This idea can be applied

by establishing rapport and looking for areas of agreement with other people.

7. Authority: This is one behavior that is most likely to be abused because of how instinctive human responses are. Not only do people in positions of authority affect us, but also titles, attire, and other symbols of power. According to one experiment, people were more likely to honk at expensive cars than at cheaper ones when the former was taking longer to stop at a traffic light. The likelihood of people complying with requests from authoritative figures is higher. This idea can be applied by showcasing your knowledge or experience in a certain area.

8. Scarcity: The fear of losing something inspires people more than the hope of gaining something. When there is a sudden shift in availability or competition, things become more desirable. Words

such as "Only 2 left" or "Limited Stocks" cause the brain to suddenly value the item more. Open art auctions and acquisitions bidding wars are two more excellent examples. Scarcity is a powerful tool for inspiring people to act; for example, by emphasizing the limited supply of a good or service.

9. Express your approval. "Call me on Thursday" and "Please get in touch with me at any time" are not the same. The person you're speaking with won't understand you and thus won't be able to fulfill your desires.

10. Have assurance. People will notice and react if you genuinely believe in what you're doing. They will aspire to have your level of confidence. It is really in your best interest to pretend to be someone you're not. Nobody needs to know that you're wearing a rental suit

when you enter a five-star restaurant. Nobody questions you as long as you don't arrive wearing jeans and a T-shirt. Think along those same lines when you present your pitch.

11. Master the art of body language. Be receptive. Maintain an open arms stance and a body that faces the other person. Make sure not to fidget, smile, and maintain good eye contact. Again, people like people who they think are similar to them; if you mirror someone, you are actually in their shoes. Lean on the elbow that mirrors theirs if they are doing so. Lean back if they do so. You should do this almost instinctively if you're feeling a rapport, so avoid doing it in a way that will draw attention to it.

12. Have tenacity. The person who is willing to persist in asking for what they want,

even in the face of persistent rejection, is the most persuasive.

In the end, the best strategy for persuasion and influence over others will vary depending on the circumstances and the subject of the influence. The probability of success can be raised by combining these concepts. Gaining an effective understanding and application of these principles will help you persuade others more successfully. But it's crucial to employ persuasion sensibly and ethically.

Chapter 2

Crafting Compelling Narratives: The Heart of Persuasive Selling

A. The Transition from Features to Advantages

Let's say you are a salesperson for household cleaning supplies. It may be your first impulse to draw attention to the product's eco-friendliness, simplicity of use, and ingredients. These are the features that your cleaning product provides, after all. But, everything changes when you change your viewpoint and concentrate on the result.

Consider the following instead of just emphasizing the technical features of your cleaning product: Instead of cleaning supplies, market immaculate homes.

This change in viewpoint highlights the transformation your customers can experience through the use of your product.

Your marketing efforts can be revitalized by switching the focus from the features of your product to the desired outcome. This will make your message more relatable and persuasive to your target audience. Recall that by emphasizing the result rather than just the process, you can establish a stronger emotional connection with your clients and increase the appeal of your goods and services.

B. Utilize Emotions

Knowing that people make decisions about what to buy based on feelings and then use logic to support those decisions is one of the keys to writing effective copy. You're speaking straight to your audience's emotional needs and desires when you put too much emphasis on the result.

Imagine creating a message that speaks to the emotional need for a tidy, hospitable, and well-organized home. You are addressing the desire for a place of comfort and pride by showcasing a sparkling home as the ultimate result of using your cleaning product.

Customers who buy from you aren't buying a bottle of cleaner; rather, they are investing in the idea of having a shining, happy home. Your cleaning product becomes a tool to help them realize their goals by highlighting the transformation that it enables.

C. Persuasive Storytelling: An Art Form

Stories have a special ability to enthrall, uplift, and forge emotional bonds. The use of narratives as persuasive techniques is effective in the field of sales. When expertly crafted, they turn commonplace goods or services into unforgettable experiences that let even strangers see the positive effects on their lives.

Persuading your audience to believe what you're saying requires an understanding of persuasive storytelling techniques. It involves creating an assortment of connected tales that take your audience on a journey. Get the audience's attention right away to draw them into the story. Every narrative segment ought to have a distinct objective that directs them toward a compelling takeaway.

Never forget that a story needs to flow naturally to keep the audience interested and get them to the desired ending. A gripping tale, after all, keeps travelers captivated and involved in the experience. When applied effectively, this strategy can boost the effect of your concluding call to action.

Apple is known for its carefully planned narrative flow in its product releases. They pique curiosity, expose traits, and evoke emotions before pleading with them to purchase their newest creation. Thus, the ability to tell a compelling story can have an impact on decisions.

Good storytelling transcends the specifications and cost of a product. It tells a story that captures the imagination of strangers and arouses feelings and desires. Salespeople are storytellers extraordinaire. They find relatable situations, add a dash of aspiration and transformation, and then delicately position their product or service as the answer to the needs or problems of strangers. Strangers can understand and feel the value proposition through stories, which makes the sales pitch memorable and effective.

D. Customer Success Stories are Highlighted

Happy customers have the potential to become real-life heroes and powerful brand ambassadors. This occurs each time they make a sincere recommendation because doing so raises your credibility and inspires trust in potential customers. When prospects witness how your products or services have benefited others, they will be able to relate to your stories. It inspires them to envision themselves utilizing your brand successfully. Customer success stories, which emphasize real results over sales language, also help to humanize your company. These stories stir emotions and show how much you truly care.

Sincerity is well received by audiences, and there are plenty of instances to choose from. Consider the "Stories from the Airbnb Community" campaign, which is run by Airbnb. This campaign showcased a range of passenger experiences to highlight the transformative power of travel. Airbnb was able to inspire others to travel confidently by putting its customers first. Customer success stories are unquestionably one of the important assets you should have in your marketing toolbox. By featuring real customers as the main characters in your stories, you can persuade potential customers to become loyal customers.

Charisma and Confidence: Bringing Out Your Inner Sales Dynamo

The intangible qualities that take a sales professional from being a presenter to a persuasive influencer are confidence and charisma. These attributes are learned via experience, education, and a sincere conviction in the benefits being provided; they are not intrinsic. Both charisma and confidence give the sales pitch authority and an enticing charm that draws in strangers.

Understanding as the Basis:

Expertise is the source of confidence. A salesperson who is knowledgeable about their product or service emanates confidence by nature. They are well-versed in the characteristics, advantages, and special selling points. With this knowledge, they feel more confident in the eyes of strangers as they can respond to any inquiry, deal with concerns, and offer insightful commentary.

The Influence of Genuineness:

Frequently misinterpreted as an exterior characteristic, charisma is a genuine manifestation of zeal and love. A magnetic aura emanating from authenticity draws in strangers. Authentic salespeople exude confidence in the value they bring to the table. They establish a human connection with strangers by showing empathy, attentive listening, and sincere concern for their needs. Sincerity like this fosters trust, which increases the strangers' openness to the sales pitch.

Body Language and Verbal Expression:
Nonverbal clues are another way to convey charisma and confidence. Sustaining eye contact, assuming a welcoming and open stance, and making deliberate gestures all contribute to the persuasive effect. In a similar vein, vocal inflection, pitch, and cadence affect how the message is understood. A self-assured, charming salesperson modulates their voice, highlighting important details and adding energy to create a lively and captivating dialogue.

To sum up, selling to strangers is an art that combines psychology, skillful storytelling, and building charisma and confidence. Persuasive selling is built on the understanding of strangers' minds, creating emotionally charged narratives, and projecting genuine confidence and charisma. Salespeople who grasp and integrate these components into their approach can impact strangers, converting them into devoted clients and transforming transactions into deep connections.

Chapter 3

Targeting the Right Strangers: Identifying Your Ideal Customer Profiles

As in life, you can't please everyone in the business. It is costly, time-consuming, and unproductive to try to make your product or service do everything. It also doesn't increase customer lifetime value. Knowing your target audience is crucial when creating a marketing campaign, as it prevents you from squandering expensive resources. What then does ICP mean in marketing? You can always know who your campaigns are targeting when you have an ideal customer profile (ICP).

Consider yourself shopping for gifts and not knowing who you are buying them for. You have to invest time, money, and energy into a gift for which you are unsure of the recipient's preferences. It doesn't seem like a very enjoyable activity. Similar to choosing gifts, you must identify your target audience before you launch a marketing campaign. That is the significance of your ICP.

ICP: What is it?

Based on firmographic and technographic information gathered at the company level (e.g., employee size, technologies utilized, industry, and so forth), an ideal customer profile represents the clients and potential clients you think will benefit the most from your offering. The first step towards revenue-driven marketing is defining your ICP.

Advantages of an ICP

Ideal customer profiles offer several indisputable benefits, as you will discover when you begin to learn what ICP stands for in marketing. We're going to go over four advantages of having an ideal client profile today that you won't want to miss:

1. Recognize your target market and create personas

You might be curious about how ICP marketing can benefit you. Knowing who you're selling to is one of the biggest advantages of an ideal customer profile. Every business has a target customer base that will most benefit from its goods and services; identifying this group will make your work much easier. Once you have a perfect customer profile, you can start researching this made-up company further to find and develop buyer personas. By using these personas, you can make your ideal customer profile come to life and learn more about the businesses and people you're marketing your brand to.

2. Targeted advertising campaigns

You can create targeted marketing campaigns that appeal to your ideal customers once you have a better understanding of your audience thanks to your ideal customer profile. Even better, you can use those campaigns to target high-value leads. The customer insights from your ideal customer profiles can be used to target your marketing campaigns, whether they are focused on search engine advertising, social media, or more conventional approaches.

For instance, businesses that advertise on social media sites like Facebook and Instagram can access analytics pages and advanced reporting. Advertisers can incorporate targeting features into their campaigns to ensure that the right people see their messaging by using these business pages. Creating an ideal customer profile is the first step towards identifying the "right" people to target.

3. Better development of goods and services

Improved development of products and services is another advantage of having an ideal client profile. You can determine the needs and desires of the people you're selling to when you start your ICP marketing by having a deeper understanding of them. Being able to foresee future issues and their solutions allows you to get a head start on creating goods or services that will satisfy those demands.

When your clients realize they have a problem that needs to be fixed, your company will be in a great position to offer a solution. By doing this, you highlight the worth and dependability of your brand. These are important qualities that consumers seek out in businesses and that can draw in devoted clients.

4. Enhanced lead generation

Improved lead conversion rates are perhaps the greatest advantage of developing an ideal client profile, and they are largely attributed to the other benefits mentioned above: persona development, targeted advertising, and better product development. To refresh your memory, your conversion rate is the proportion of visitors who finish the desired action. It refers to the proportion of leads and prospects that you convert into paying clients in this instance.

Knowing your target market can help you develop marketing campaigns that are more focused and gain a deeper understanding of the needs and desires of your customers. With this knowledge, you can keep developing and providing solutions that will better serve your clients. You can also determine which leads are most profitable at the same time and focus your campaigns on them. These steps increase the effectiveness of sales efforts and campaigns, which raises lead conversion rates.

How to Design an Effective ICP

Now that we've discussed the What and Why of ideal customer profiles, let's examine the How. Continue reading for a step-by-step tutorial on developing the perfect customer profile that will enable you to comprehend and establish a connection with your target market.

1. Gather information from your present clientele.

Collecting information from your present clientele is the first step towards developing the perfect customer profile. You will utilize this information to make data-driven decisions regarding your customers' behavior.

In particular, you ought to give your "best" clients more consideration. These are the people you consistently and successfully sell to. In the following steps, your best clients will play a crucial role in assisting you in developing the perfect customer profile.

2. Examine the information for any patterns or parallels.

It's time to analyze your customer data after you've collected it.

You want to look into the data for any patterns or similarities that point to any recurring themes or behaviors, especially among your best clients. (PSSST: Nutshell's reporting tools allow you to look for trends in your customer data!).

Look for distinguishing qualities in your customers, such as:

- Business
- Location geographically
- Income or revenue
- company size and organization

3. Review your conclusions.

Examine the patterns you identified in the preceding stage — what catches your attention? Think about inquiries such as:

- Do these businesses operate in the same or comparable industries?
- Which area do these businesses operate in?
- What is the typical number of employees?
- Are there particular goods or services that are used or bought more frequently?

The framework of your ideal customer profile will be built by taking note of and keeping in mind the traits that your customer base shares in common.

4. Establish your ICP.

After completing a thorough investigation of your present customers and the firmographic traits they have in common, you can start assembling the results into a single master document. This will turn into the perfect client profile for you. Now that you have outlined all of your research, start developing the profile of your ideal client. This made-up business will be the result of everything you gleaned from your previous research.

To truly understand your audience, you can now go a step further and begin creating buyer personas inside of your ideal client profile.
Here are a few fundamental inquiries to get you going:

- Who are your clients at the moment? Who has purchased from you already?
- Do you want to change your focus or do you want to keep going after the same people?
- Justify any changes you make to your customer focus. Why specifically do you wish to focus on a different clientele? What will this achieve for your company?

- How did your current clients learn about your company?
- Right now, who gains the most from your product or service? Explain them.
- What particular issue or difficulty is your product or service helping these people with?
- What kind of feedback have you received from your current clientele?
- Who was it that you specifically intended to assist when you launched this business?
- Do those individuals currently make purchases from you? Why not, if not?

ICP optimal procedures

After you've created your ideal customer profile, there's still work to be done. Review some best practices to keep your profile up to date.

A. Speak with your clients.

Don't ignore your customers because they are the lifeblood of your ideal customer profile! Engage in conversation with your clients whenever you can to learn more about them and obtain additional insightful information that will help you refine your ideal client profile. You can get important information from your customers that you might not find with simple data analysis.

Keeping in touch with your customers can help you stay in touch with your audience as a whole, not to mention that your ideal customer profile will help you attract new clients.

B. Check in with your ICP frequently.

Keeping in touch aside, reviewing and updating your ideal customer profile regularly is another crucial best practice. Your ideal customer profile should evolve along with the shifting interests, routines, and needs of your audience. To make sure your ideal customer profile is current and appropriately represents your target market, it's a good idea to review it regularly.

Precision in Demographics: Crafting the Ideal Customer Portrait

Consider your perfect client. Are they parents looking for family-friendly solutions, or are they young professionals looking for convenience? You can outline the fundamental characteristics of your audience using the broad strokes provided by demographics. These characteristics help you create the first picture of your ideal client: age, gender, income level, and location.

A. **Age and Life Stage:** Knowing your audience's various life stages is like knowing a book's chapters. Every stage has its own special difficulties, goals, and purchasing habits. For example, retirees may value stability and dependability more than young adults, who may be more receptive to technological innovations. Understanding these variations will enable you to customize your offerings to meet particular needs, increasing the appeal and relevance of your goods and services.

B. **Gender and Lifestyle:** Decisions made regarding lifestyle and gender dynamics have a significant impact on consumer behavior. A married man in the same age group may have different priorities than a thirty-something single woman. Lifestyle decisions, including exercise regimens, pastimes, and spending patterns, enhance the portrait. By taking note of these distinctions, you can develop audience-specific marketing campaigns that connect with them based on common goals and experiences.

Geography is more than just a dot on a map; it's a cultural mosaic that shapes values and preferences. Location also has an impact on culture. While people in rural areas may seek community and sustainability, urban dwellers may prioritize speed and convenience. Strangers' perceptions and interactions with goods and services are influenced by cultural quirks, customs, and regional events. By embracing these cultural influences, you can make your marketing strategies appealing to your audience and help them feel like they belong.

Psychographic Insights: Perceiving the Values and Lifestyles of Strangers

Psychographics is a complex field that goes beyond basic demographics. Consider it as painting your canvas with colors and giving your ideal client profiles more nuance and character. Psychographics provide you with a comprehensive understanding of your audience by delving into the nuances of values, beliefs, interests, and lifestyles.

A. **Values and Beliefs:** Your audience's values and beliefs act as a compass to help them make decisions. Do they value sustainability and the environment? Do they give social causes and community involvement priority? Knowing these guiding principles enables you to connect your brand with causes that are significant to your target market. Sharing common values with others not only forges a deeper bond but also gives them a sense of direction, turning them from total strangers into devoted supporters.

B. **Interests and Hobbies:** People's passions and interests are the threads that bind their lives together. These interests, which might include technology, fitness, travel, or the arts, capture the essence of your target audience. You can make deeply meaningful immersive experiences by matching your offerings with these passions. It becomes a shared journey that improves your customers' lives and makes them feel more connected to your brand than just a transaction.

C. **Aspirations and Difficulties:** Every person has goals and encounters difficulties. As a company, you can present your goods and services as enablers and solutions by being aware of these aspirations and challenges. Whether the objectives of your clients are enhanced well-being, financial security, or personal development, your products and services can act as the sparkplugs that enable them to reach their objectives. You meet their needs and contribute significantly to their success stories by showing empathy for their difficulties and offering sincere solutions.

Chapter 4

Building Irresistible Offers: Creating Value that Strangers Can't Resist

You must comprehend the emotional triggers and desired transformation of your potential customers if you hope to make an offer that they won't be able to refuse. You can identify these triggers by conducting buyer persona research. After that, all you need to do is demonstrate to them how you'll bring about that change.

Many people think that developing a compelling offer requires having a unique product. That is just untrue. Even the dullest product can be made into an enticing offer. Focusing on your customer rather than boasting about yourself is the secret to making a successful offer. Demonstrate to them how your product can help them get from one place to another.

Let's take an example where you provide small business owners with business coaching. You are aware that potential clients wish to expand their businesses, but they are unsure of how to go about doing so. They also worry about squandering money and making poor choices."I'll help grow your business by 30 percent in the next six months with my proven system," could be your marketing pitch. I'll refund your money if you're not satisfied with the outcome. If your offer is customized for your target audience, you have a higher chance of receiving a yes.

The psychology of a compelling proposal
Contrary to popular belief, people do not base their decisions on the truth. We use reasoning to support the decisions we make, which are based primarily on our feelings. When developing your

message, it is crucial to comprehend what makes an irresistible offer. Let's look more closely at some psychological triggers that you can employ to craft an offer that is too good to refuse:

A. Scarcity

Social proof is indirectly produced by scarcity. People are more inclined to purchase the product before it sells out when they get the impression that an offer is well-liked or quickly selling out. It's an effective marketing tool that can increase the appeal of your offers. If you are selling event tickets, for instance, you may state that there are only a certain quantity of tickets available.

Other phrases that imply scarcity include "limited edition," "selling fast," and "only x number left." These words compel people to act quickly by fostering a sense of urgency. This is demonstrated on the Booking.com website. The number of rooms left is shown in a bold red font.

B. Haste The fear of missing out, or FOMO

FOMO is the emotion that arises when someone fears missing out on something. When you create a sense of urgency, FOMO is the psychological trigger that pushes people to purchase your goods. While scarcity and urgency are closely associated, scarcity is not the only factor that influences urgency. Other strategies, such as time-sensitive offers, flash sales, early bird specials, or exclusive access to content, can be used to create urgency. Amazon is utilizing it on its homepage. Each product has a countdown timer on it as well.

C. Utilize social proof to establish trust

The idea behind social proof is straightforward: people are more inclined to take action themselves when they observe others taking it. The bandwagon effect is real. And social proof is a useful tool for crafting an offer that is too good to refuse. Social evidence can take the shape of client endorsements, contented social media posts, or even anecdotes about your past charitable work.

Tony Robbins accomplishes this on his website by featuring endorsements from Salesforce CEO Marc Benioff, professional tennis player Serena Williams, and TV host and actress Maria Menounos. Another way to create social proof for an established brand is to list the number of customers you have taken care of or publish press releases about your company in the media.

D. Reduce Resistance

Making it simple for your clients to accept your offer will raise your conversion rate and improve your financial results. How therefore can you make your offers less frictional? Here are a few easy methods to lower barriers to entry:

- Ensure that your offer is understandable and unambiguous. Steer clear of jargon and speak clearly.

- Provide all necessary details upfront. Avoid making your clients look for information.

- Take down any obstacles to acceptance. Remove anything that might be preventing your customers from taking advantage of your offer.

- Make the decision-making process simpler. Assist your clients in weighing the advantages and disadvantages so they can decide swiftly and sensibly.

- Respond to objections beforehand. If you can foresee the objections from your clients, take them up in your offer.

- Give payment schedules. Allow your clients to make flexible payment arrangements.
- Offer assistance to customers. Make sure you have a representative on hand to respond to inquiries from clients.

E. Amplify the perceived worth

Perceived value is critical in sales negotiations. Your offer will be more alluring the more value your customer feels it offers. Two excellent strategies to increase perceived value and make your offer irresistible are bonuses and offer stacking.

Extra goods or services that you include along with your main offer are known as bonuses. They should be something your customer would want or need, but they don't have to be costly or complicated. For instance, if you're offering a course on how to launch a business, your bonus might be a list of resources or templates for a business plan.

When you combine several goods or services into a single offer, this is known as offer stacking or value stacking. Because it gives your customer more value for their money, this is a great way to raise the perceived value of your offer.

If you are marketing a fitness program, for instance, your value stack might resemble this:

- Setting goals during a 30-minute Zoom session with the trainer
- A 30-day diet regimen to maintain high levels of energy
- A regimen for working out at home
- access to a closed Facebook group for inspiration and guidance
- individual email assistance
- Entry to the closed Facebook group for members only

- Special savings on supplements and additional consultations

F. Hazard Reversal

Using a technique known as "risk reversal," you can make your offer less risky so that your buyer can purchase with assurance. There are two options for finishing this task:

- Make a money-back promise available. Because it removes all risk from your customer, this is one of the most popular methods for risk reduction. They can get a refund if they're not satisfied with the goods or service.

- Just pay for what you enjoy. This is a fantastic method for lowering the danger for internet buyers. They can return the item for a refund if they're not satisfied with it when they receive it.

- Give it a trial run. This is a fantastic method of lowering the risk associated with subscription services. Before they are charged, your customer has a limited amount of time to test out the service.

G. Make your deal stand out.

Ever wonder why some offers seem too good to refuse while others are unacceptably bad? It frequently has to do with how special the deal is. Your offer will be more persuasive and alluring if it is made unique. To that end, here are a few methods:

- Promote a cause: You can access a potent source of motivation when you stand up for something greater than yourself. In addition to making your offer more appealing, you'll draw in like-minded clients by associating your brand with a cause.

- Make a sound: What sets you apart from the rest of the pack? This could be your personality, style, or niche. By speaking up, you demonstrate to others that you are a real person they can trust.

- Show off your experience and USP: What do you have to give that others don't? Make sure to include any special knowledge or abilities you may have in your offer. This could be anything from having the most cutting-edge technology to having the most experienced team. One example of the business's USP is the seamless integration of all Microsoft apps. Others are unable to simply duplicate it.

A good illustration of a business supporting a cause is TOMS. TOMS will provide a child in need with a pair of shoes for each purchase you make. They've increased the persuasiveness and customer appeal of their offer by tying their brand to a cause.

H. Fix the price.

Everyone loves it a lot. Amazing deals are difficult to pass up and can be an effective marketing strategy. However, a lot of people are unaware of the fact that making an offer that is hard to refuse is only as important as choosing the appropriate price.

Making offers that are too good to refuse doesn't mean offering your product for free or drastically reducing its price. The key is to identify the sweet spot, where your price is both high enough to turn a profit and low enough to entice potential customers. You can identify this sweet spot by experimenting with different prices.

To determine the best pricing strategy for your target audience, you must first understand them.

Products that demand a premium price include fine wine, designer clothing, and Apple products. However, how do they manage to charge so much? It's because they have done their homework and are aware that the people in their target market are prepared to pay more for higher-quality products. Conversely, fast-food establishments such as Burger King and McDonald's employ a value-based pricing approach. They set their prices low to draw clients because they are aware that their target market is price-sensitive.

Finding the ideal ratio between price and value is essential if you want to make an offer that people can't resist. Additionally, you must comprehend your target market's spending power about your good or service.

I.   Temporary Offers

The feeling of time running out is a strong incentive. Limited-time deals instill a sense of urgency in strangers, encouraging them to act before the chance passes them by. Whether you're running a countdown timer on your website, a flash sale, or a 24-hour discount, you have to make decisions quickly. To seal a deal that might never come back, strangers are more likely to move quickly.

J. Exclusive Offers and Invite-Only Deals

Invite-only promotions satisfy the desire for exclusivity. Strangers become more devoted and engaged when they perceive themselves as members of an exclusive group with access to exclusive offers. A select group of clients or subscribers can receive exclusive offers, which will make them feel appreciated. Because it is exclusive to a select few, there is a pressing need to take advantage of the opportunity.

K. Psychological Pricing

Pricing strategies based on psychological factors can influence people's thoughts. Purchase decisions are influenced by subtleties such as the allure of a "limited time offer," the charm of paying $9.99 rather than $10.00, or the status that comes with paying a premium price. You can make an offer seem not just reasonable but also irresistible by setting prices that appeal to your customers' emotions by understanding psychological triggers.

In summary, Pricing tactics, bonus offers, urgency, and scarcity are the cornerstones that hold up your alluring proposition in the world of irresistible offers. By striking the ideal balance between affordability and value, adding alluring bonuses to the package, and deftly using scarcity and urgency, you can create a magnetic pull that draws people in and turns them from onlookers into eager buyers. It's an art to make an offer that strangers can't refuse, and you can make every encounter into a compelling opportunity by combining psychology and creativity in just the right amounts. So go ahead and add value to your offers, make sure your call to action (CTA) is obvious, and watch as strangers enthusiastically accept what you have to offer—allowing your business to grow in the process.

Chapter 5

Stranger to Advocate: Building Long-Term Relationships Through Exceptional Service

Few things have as much of an impact on your business as poor customer service, both negatively and positively. Long-term clients and repeat business can result from a positive experience. Unhappy customers lose revenue, and even negative public relations can result from a poor customer experience. Even so, a lot of companies still have trouble providing excellent customer service. Building relationships with both prospective and current clients enables companies to provide a more appealing and customized customer experience. Furthermore, the success of your business in the long run will depend entirely on the caliber of the experience you provide.

According to a recent study, 86% of consumers say their experiences are just as significant as the goods or services they buy. This means that in addition to offering the goods and services that consumers require, businesses also must provide an excellent end-to-end experience at every touchpoint.

Creating WOW Moments: The Cornerstone of Customer Support

Imagine entering an environment where each encounter with a customer is more than just a business transaction—rather, it is a memorable one. This is what it means to deliver WOW experiences—a philosophy that goes beyond simple satisfaction to the point of delight and amazement.

- **Recognizing Needs and Wants:** Creating WOW experiences starts with a thorough understanding of your clients. It involves assuming their needs and wants before they express them. You can proactively provide solutions that surpass their expectations by demonstrating empathy for their challenges and aspirations. These delightful moments, whether they are in the form of a personalized recommendation, an unexpected bonus, or a kind deed, leave a lasting impression and help you develop a strong emotional bond with your clients.

- **Making Memorable Touchpoints:** You have the chance to create a WOW moment at every customer touchpoint. These little things count, whether it's the smooth operation of your website, the friendliness of your customer support team, or the sophistication of your packaging. Paying attention to even the smallest details shows that you are committed to giving customers an exceptional experience. A personalized thank-you note, an unexpected birthday discount, or a follow-up call to make sure they're satisfied are small touches that take an ordinary customer experience to a whole new level.

- **Handling Conflict with Grace:** Errors and problems are unavoidable, but how you respond to them determines how you interact with your clients. Having a WOW experience is more than just doing transactions perfectly; it's also about handling problems with grace. When a negative situation is resolved quickly and sympathetically and is accompanied by genuine apologies and compensatory actions, it can be turned into a chance to gain the customer's trust and loyalty. Consumers recall both the mistake and the correction process.

Good Customer Feedback Loops: Paying Attention to and Acquiring Knowledge from Your Proponents

The exchange of feedback is essential to progress. Successful customer feedback loops are how you receive, process, and apply knowledge. Your supporters are more than simply clients; they are priceless sources of information that have the power to influence your company's future.

- **Active Listening and Empathy:** Listening is more than just hearing; it's also about comprehending and feeling the viewpoints of your clients. Regardless of the type of feedback received from customers, actively engage with them. Every comment is a window into their expectations and experiences. You establish rapport and show that you care about their happiness by listening to their worries and valuing their compliments.

- **Culture of Continuous Improvement:** Seeing feedback as a growth-promoting catalyst is the first step toward creating a culture of continuous improvement. Examine feedback patterns to find reoccurring problems or compliments. Make better use of this data to improve your services, streamline your operations, and improve your products. The feedback loop is a proactive tool for innovation rather than merely a reactive one. Initiate brainstorming sessions with your team based on feedback from customers. Encourage a culture where all team members are involved in improving the customer experience.

- **Surveys and Feedback Tools:** Use surveys and feedback tools to methodically collect structured feedback.

With surveys, you can ask targeted questions and find out what your customers think about different areas of your company. Quantitative data can be obtained through online feedback forms, email surveys, or social media polls to supplement qualitative feedback. You can make data-driven decisions by integrating both structured and unstructured feedback to obtain a thorough grasp of customer perceptions.

Programs for Loyalty and Retention: Maintaining Happy and Involved Advocates

More than just point systems, loyalty programs are tactical tools that foster connections, recognize and reward loyalty, and promote repeat business. Conversely, retention strategies concentrate on making sure that your advocates continue to be happy and involved in the long run.

- Tailored Loyalty Programs: Highly effective loyalty programs are those that align with the interests and habits of your target audience. Consider the interests of your advocates when designing your loyalty programs. For example, if your target market is interested in experiences, think about providing workshops or special events. If they enjoy freebies and discounts, design your loyalty program so that members can earn rewards by accruing points. The secret is to make sure your advocates see real value in their involvement by matching the program with what drives them.

- Personalized Recognition and Awards: The key to successful retention is personalization. Refer to your advocates by name, take note of their past purchases, and personalize your correspondence according to their interests. Personalized offers and special discounts when it comes to rewards foster a feeling of appreciation and exclusivity. Personalized gestures, like birthday gifts, special anniversary discounts, or early access to upcoming products, strengthen the relationship between your brand and its advocates.

- Social Proof and Community Engagement: Creating a community around your brand makes people feel like they belong. Membership sites, social media groups, and online forums offer areas for interaction, experience sharing, and bonding amongst your advocates who are passionate about your goods or services. Promote user-generated content, including product reviews, testimonies, and images of the products in use. Positive customer reviews and anecdotes from happy customers serve as social proof, which builds brand credibility and sways potential customers in the direction of advocacy and trust.

How does a Customer Value Journey appear?
It's common knowledge that if you ask someone how they're doing right away and then ask them if they want to spend the rest of their lives together, your chances of success in a human relationship are extremely slim. It's probably going to set off a rather abrupt and unwanted reaction. What are the chances of getting a second date if you manage to get a date but spend the entire time gushing about how amazing you are and how much the other person needs you? In what way might a business relationship be any different? It isn't. Meeting potential prospects where they are and providing for their needs will be more intentional if you are

aware of the steps involved in building a relationship, whether it be personal or professional. The customer value journey stages listed below are meant to help your ideal client go from being a naive prospect to an enthusiastic promoter.

Step 1: Awareness

The qualifying prospects' initial exposure to your brand, goods, or services is characterized by the Awareness stage. To get a click or visit, you want to leave an impression. This could happen through organic search, paid search, display, social boost, billboards, bus wraps, and so forth, or paid advertising.

Step 2: Participate

Engage concentrates on gaining a prospect's attention and trust while awareness campaigns drive views and clicks. This is frequently done through content marketing, such as blog posts,

FAQs, relevant case studies on your website, or posts on social media platforms like Facebook, LinkedIn, or YouTube.

Step 3: Enroll

When you get to the "Subscribe" stage, the potential customer has decided your material is interesting and wants to hear from you further. Some level of trust has been earned by you. It's time to offer something of greater value in exchange for the prospect's contact information and consent to contact them again through marketing. This might come in the form of a newsletter, on-demand webinar, blog subscription, or content download.

Step 4: Convert

In this instance, the potential customer is offering a financial or time commitment in return for a good or service. This might be an agreement to attend a consultation, a product trial, or an informational meeting in a business-to-business setting. Often referred to as an entry-level offer, the value of the good or service might vary substantially. Creating an opportunity to excite your prospect is the aim of the concert stage.

Step 5: Excited

Excite is your chance to show a potential customer how your good or service transforms from a nice-to-have to a necessary or highly desired item. The product demo function, the slide in the deck that prospects want to see repeatedly, and the ROI calculator that they ask you to share with their executive team are the things that they can't bear to lose after 30 days. Being intentional about this phase of the journey is essential to marketing and sales success because it's during these "Ah-Ha" moments that the real breakthroughs occur on both sides of the relationship.

Step 6: Ascend

Your customers will be keen to make sure they have access to your necessary product or service now that the worth of it has been confirmed. The Ascend stage, which is sometimes represented as a ladder, describes your primary or core offering along with other pertinent offers you make that continue to add value after the first sale. Increasing client value and satisfaction is the aim of the Ascend stage.

Step 7: Advocate

You have been cultivating long-term customer satisfaction, providing value, and establishing trust throughout the journey thus far. A satisfied client should be your reward if you are successful. Additionally, these satisfied clients probably know other satisfied clients who would be happy to recommend you. To raise awareness, trust, and credibility with a wider audience, the Advocate stage formalizes the process of developing customer advocates who are eager to spread the word about their positive experiences.

Step 8: Advertise

Building brand advocates who actively market to their audience on your behalf is the main goal of the Promote stage. This can be in the form of incentives, affiliate or referral schemes, or simply making it simple for contented clients to brag about you. Brand ambassadors provide recommendations from a reliable source whether they are paid or not, which frequently lowers your customer acquisition expenses.

Developing relationships with customers is an essential corporate goal everywhere. Provide your customers with reasons to emotionally connect with your brand if you want to increase brand engagement. It is practically necessary to go beyond customer relationship management (CRM) and implement strategies for creating and preserving positive client relationships. When you have the right tools and customer relationship strategies, it will help you strengthen your relationships with customers and create a strong foundation that will help you grow your business to new heights.

Chapter 6

Adapt or Perish: Handling the Changing Sales and Marketing Environment

In today's business world, there are essentially only two options: adapt or perish. Companies that don't adapt to the changing times will quickly find it harder to compete and fall behind. Businesses that adapt to the latest trends and technologies and are constantly changing are the ones that thrive. They are the ones who don't mind taking chances and trying new things. So what does it take for a company to be successful in the contemporary world? Above all, you need to be adaptive and flexible. It's necessary to embrace change rather than resist it. In the world of business, change is the only constant, so you have to be prepared for it.

Second, you need to be willing to take chances. If you want to succeed, you have to be willing to try new things and experiment. Failure is a necessary part of the process and is therefore inevitable. Additionally, you should never stop learning. Because the business world is ever-evolving, you have to constantly learn new things. Stay up to date with the latest technological advancements and trends, and never stop looking for new ways to improve your business.

Finally, you need to put together a capable team. Gather around you a group of bright, creative, and passionate people. These people will lead you to success by guiding you through the ever-changing terrain. If you can focus on these four areas, you'll flourish in today's business world. So why do you wait? Get out there and start adjusting!

Technologies and Trends: Following the Sales Curve

In the digital age, adopting new technologies and following trends is now a need rather than a choice. The way businesses engage with their target market is being altered by new technologies, which is causing a rapid change in the sales and marketing industry. To stay ahead of the curve, businesses must not only adjust to these changes but also anticipate emerging trends.

- Taking E-Commerce and Mobile Platforms: The advent of mobile platforms and e-commerce has brought about a significant shift in consumer purchasing behavior. Customers' preference for the convenience of shopping on smartphones and tablets is rising as a result of the widespread use of mobile devices. Businesses need to optimize their online presence for mobile platforms to ensure easy navigation and seamless user experiences. You can broaden your customer base and profit from the growing trend of online shopping by embracing e-commerce.

- Getting the Most Out of Social Media: In addition to being a platform for social interaction, social media is an effective tool for marketing and sales. Social media platforms like Instagram, Facebook, Twitter, and LinkedIn not only serve as venues for brand promotion but also offer a direct channel of contact with consumers. Businesses need to create compelling social media strategies that resonate with their audience. Social media platforms provide businesses with multiple avenues for interaction and connection: engaging posts on Facebook, visually stunning content on Instagram, business networking on LinkedIn, and interactive posts on Facebook.

- Examining Artificial Intelligence and Chatbots: Not just a catchphrase, artificial intelligence (AI) is revolutionizing sales and customer service. Artificial intelligence (AI)-enabled chatbots are capable of handling transactions, answering customer inquiries, and providing personalized recommendations in real-time. Businesses can use AI to assess customer data, predict purchase trends, and enhance the overall customer experience. By incorporating AI technologies, businesses can increase productivity, save time, and offer more specialized and focused services to their clients.

Cultural Intelligence: Adapting Your Conduct through a Variety of Social Interactions

In today's globalized world, cultural sensitivity and understanding are critical for sales and marketing campaigns to be successful. Beyond just identifying cultural differences, cultural intelligence involves leveraging them to create deep connections with a varied clientele.

- Respecting cultural traditions and conventions: Different cultures have different taboos, conventions, and customs. Some cultures find certain things acceptable while others find them offensive. Businesses need to invest time and resources to understand the nuanced cultural differences of their target market. Marketing strategies should be guided by this data, as well as product offerings and customer interactions. Companies that respect cultural norms and demonstrate their cultural competency win the confidence and business of a diverse clientele.

- Localization of Language and Communication: Language is a powerful tool for forming relationships with various strangers. In addition to translation, language localization requires a deep understanding of cultural contexts and nuances. Businesses should invest in professional translation services to ensure that their marketing materials and communications are culturally sensitive and linguistically accurate. To effectively bridge language gaps, businesses should also consider hiring bilingual staff members or interpreters.

- Marketing Initiatives that Respect Diversity: It is vital to be represented. Diverse consumers find campaigns promoting inclusive marketing that celebrates diversity appealing. A range of faces, cultures, and lifestyles are featured in advertisements and promotional materials, which makes customers from diverse backgrounds feel noticed and valued. This is not just a reflection of the world as it is. Inclusive marketing campaigns foster a sense of belonging and inspire individuals from diverse backgrounds to develop a personal relationship with the brand.

Agile Marketing: Modifying Strategies in Response to Market Developments

Companies that are successful in a rapidly evolving market need to be agile. Agile marketing refers to the ability to quickly modify plans in response to shifting consumer trends, market shifts, or new trends. All it takes is imagination, flexibility, and a willingness to view change as an opportunity rather than a danger.

❖ Real-time data analysis and decision-making: In the digital age, businesses have an abundance of data at their disposal. Agile marketing tracks new consumer trends, preferences, and behaviors by analyzing data in real time. Employing data analytics tools enables businesses to make well-informed decisions quickly. Real-time insights enable businesses to spot new opportunities, spot possible issues, and quickly adjust their strategies.

❖ Fast Idea Prototyping and Testing: Agile marketing encourages rapid prototyping and idea testing. Instead of spending months planning a large-scale marketing campaign, businesses can create small-scale prototypes or trial campaigns. Because these prototypes are released quickly, businesses can get real-time customer feedback. By considering the feedback, businesses can refine their strategies, expand the successful ones, and improve their campaigns. By using rapid prototyping to shorten the time to market for new ideas, businesses can stay one step ahead of their competitors.

- ❖ Embracing Creativity and Innovation: Agile marketing requires a high degree of creativity and invention. It encourages businesses to experiment with new ideas, creative concepts, and unconventional approaches. To embrace creativity, one must realize that there is no box at all, which requires more than just thinking creatively. Businesses can collaborate with creative individuals, set up brainstorming sessions, and host innovation challenges within their teams. By fostering a creative culture, businesses can find innovative solutions, cutting-edge marketing strategies, and fresh approaches to interacting with strangers.

In the ever-changing landscape of sales and marketing, businesses must acknowledge adaptation as a fundamental tactic for both survival and expansion. Businesses that stay ahead of trends and technologies, understand and value diverse cultures, and use agile marketing techniques can effectively manage the challenges of change and use them for innovation and prosperity. As the digital era progresses, adaptability will continue to be a critical attribute of prosperous businesses. The path to long-term success therefore lies in adapting to change, seizing diversity, and innovating without fear for entrepreneurs.

Bonus

The Unstoppable Offer Checklist & Template

You can create an offer that is too good to refuse by using these ten essential questions. Keep in mind that if something doesn't make you stop and wonder, "Am I crazy to be offering this?" In the commotion, it's probably going to be missed.

1. What are the true aspirations and pain points of my audience?

The audience comes first in marketing, just like in any other kind of communication. Take a step back here. You probably already have an idea about this; otherwise, you wouldn't be in business. A new outlook has the power to transform everything! Take a close look at their world and consider the suffering they are going through right now as well as their future objectives. What goals do they have that they are unable to currently achieve, and how might your offer assist them in achieving these goals?

2. How can I differentiate this offer from the competition?

Looking over a list of products that your rivals are offering is the next step. Pay attention to any warranties or extras they include to entice you to accept the offer. After examining roughly ten of your most formidable rivals, consider how you can outperform them in terms of value.

3. In addition to making my potential customer's life easier, how can I help them get closer to their objectives?

Ours is a fast-paced, convenient world. To see that, all you have to do is observe the expansion of Uber, Amazon, and Netflix! Never stop asking yourself how you can simplify the procedure more than your rivals. Considering that if you don't, someone else will!

4. Is it possible for me to split this offer up and make a more alluring entry-level offer?

Although they are incredibly underutilized, entry-point offers have the potential to dramatically increase your revenue and foster greater customer trust. Assume that your lowest-value offering currently costs £200. Check to see if you can separate that main offer into a smaller, more affordable offer by taking a small but valuable portion of it. By lowering the barrier to entry, you can encourage your customers to complete that crucial first transaction. This is commonly referred to as an entry-point offer. Because people are inherently skeptical, you can gain the trust of those who previously would not have given you a chance by acting in this way. Now is your chance to show them that you are capable of meeting their needs!

5. What issue do they currently wish to resolve?

Continuing from the previous point of splintering your offer, keep in mind that people often want to feel better when they first learn about a problem rather than the underlying solution. You have the chance to gain people's trust by meeting them where they are and providing them with something to ease their initial discomfort. Then, you can inform them about the benefits of your "cure."

A chiropractor who performs spinal adjustments, for instance, might consider providing a guide titled "5 ways to relieve your back pain from home." In addition to helping the client resolve their initial issue, this would establish credibility and trust. Furthermore, you can bet that when the time comes for them to purchase the entire product, they will think of this person first.

6. How can I add a BOLD guarantee or reverse the risk?

Spend some time examining each component of your product offering with a critical eye. Act as though you were considering an offer from a rival company. What kinds of uncertainties, worries, or presumptions might you have? Consider some strategies to mitigate that risk or a possible assurance you could provide to differentiate yourself from the competition.

7. Does my proposal express the transformation clearly?

Consumers purchase the changes that goods and services bring about rather than the actual goods and services themselves. Remember that you are selling more than just newly laid lawns, even if you are selling a lawnmower. You might be selling...

A feeling of accomplishment for owning the most beautiful garden on the block More family time because they can now spend less time repairing broken lawnmowers

Make sure you are communicating your potential customers' transformation in a way that reflects your complete understanding of it.

8. Do I have references or social proof that I can use?

Sometimes all it takes to have a MASSIVE impact on the expansion of your business is one or two raving fans. But as you undoubtedly know, every customer is unique! Simply put, some people are more expressive than others!

Should you accomplish the same feats for two individuals, for instance, one of them will never stop bragging about how you changed their life, while the other will merely express gratitude and write a five-star review? Locate your "raving fans" and ask them to submit a review or, if you can, a video; these can be very effective at boosting conversions. Oh, and think about launching a referral or affiliate program if you haven't already!

9. Can I apply urgency or scarcity?

Can you make your offer seem more urgent or scarce? Do you offer any goods or services that are only available in certain quantities? If so, make use of this! Making your offer seem more appealing by using scarcity can also be a very powerful strategy for boosting conversions.

10. Is my offer worth ten times what I'm asking for?

It was once stated by Russell Brunson that he uses a straightforward model to verify an offer. "Is this offer worth 10x what I'm charging for it?" he asks himself. Furthermore, charging ten times as much as everyone else doesn't suffice. Making an offer that is ten times more valuable to YOUR customer than what the competition is offering is the key. Once more, to do this, you must understand your customer avatar and what matters to them most.

The Art of Writing a Convincing Copy

You are a business owner, then. You would like to launch a brand-new offer, enroll more customers, or sell more goods. However, when it comes to actually selling your goods or services (without sounding like a car salesman), you're a little, well, stumped. You might not be familiar with the proverb "The more things change, the more they stay the same". In terms of copywriting and marketing, that adage is unquestionably accurate.

Just try to picture advertising, blogging, emails, articles, features, podcasts, scripts, and so on as a means of promoting your company. Without copywriting, your message (and the solution your audience needs!) has very little chance of reaching its intended audience if your audience—and your clients—are online. Copywriting, you see, is more than just words on a page; it's about telling a story that influences, informs, and inspires.

Understanding how to promote audience engagement and turn readers into customers is essential if you want to grow your business. This implies that you must be proficient in writing copy that grabs readers. For this reason, the copywriting process consists of the following steps:

Step 1: Determine who your audience is
Knowing your target audience is essential to writing compelling copy. The simplest way to accomplish this? Explore the minds of your audience in detail. What are their hangouts? What social media sites are they using? What are their complaints, according to them? Make thorough customer personas that include their goals, pain points, aspirations, and behaviors.

Similar to choosing a color scheme for a masterpiece, this step is fundamental.

Step 2: Carry out your study

You must conduct research; you cannot omit this step. Research is about delving deeply rather than just touching the surface. Take the time to thoroughly understand the needs of your audience by conducting in-depth research on them. Use that information to guide your discussion of the "perks" of your special offer. As you hear: You already know everything there is to know about your offer, including its features, advantages, and special selling points. However, you must match the needs of your audience with your program or product to sell it.

Their desire = your product will be the intersection point when you combine the data, statistics, and customer insights you discovered during your research with what you already know about your offer. Selling your offer is essentially effortless at that intersection. Researching your topic gives your copy the vital credibility and depth it needs, in addition to making writing your sales page, social media post, or email easier. This small gesture demonstrates to the reader that you are aware of their needs (and helps foster trust between you and your offers).

Step 3: Your grabbing headline and attention
Your key to drawing attention is a catchy headline that is easy to click on. A compelling headline captures the essence of your content, highlights the advantages of your offer, and piques readers' curiosity, encouraging them to continue reading. Try a variety of headline formats, such as provocative queries or forceful affirmations. Find the magnetic formula by testing and improving.

Step 4: Tell a Great Story

Follow me in this. I understand how alluring it is to enumerate every feature your amazing program has to offer. But I can assure you that will only make people fall asleep. Consider what drives your purchasing behavior; chances are, the benefits (or outcome) of a feature will interest you more than the feature itself.

As an illustration, let's look at shoes. You're looking for a new pair of running shoes because your current ones are trash and that particular model is no longer manufactured. Do you check the sole for the kind of foam? or as you browse Zappos or go up and down the aisles, the technical specifications of the laces?

You are undoubtedly reading a lot of reviews (and stories), even though you might not be considering those features. And why? They offer information about how your new shoes will behave, feel, and perform. For this reason, well-written copy engages and persuades by telling a story. Authentically captivating narratives center around the reader's issue or annoyance and present your proposal as the sole remedy. And when used properly, social proof—the next step—is one of the best strategies for crafting an engaging narrative.

Step Five: Social Proof

I would like you to remember this if you take anything away from reading this today: The fundamental element of persuasion is trust. Conversions are made much simpler when you use social proof.

Social proof: what is it? Case studies, endorsements, reviews, and testimonies are examples of social proof. Don't worry, though; just share your own first-hand experience if you don't yet have a library of testimonials.

Use your testimonials if you do have any to share! The greatest way to give your copy more authenticity is to hear from satisfied clients and customers about how amazing you are. It also emphasizes the advantages of your offer.

Step 6: The Essential Calls To Action

You've included social evidence, crafted a few gripping stories, and created an attention-grabbing headline. Your call to action, sometimes known as a "CTA," is the next and possibly most crucial item. What a good call to action asks the reader to do is obvious. Use "book a call" or "contact Brea," for instance, if you'd like them to schedule a call.

Alternatively, you could say "get the newsletter" or "subscribe now" to get someone to sign up for your newsletter. But when you want them to buy your offer, what about that?

Herein lies the true beauty of copywriting. In addition to offering instructions, your CTA should persuade, thrill, and reassure. The last push that converts a reader into a buyer is this one.

For instance, if you'd like to

- "Limited Time Offer – Buy Now!" will help you create a sense of urgency.
- Use a catchphrase like "Double Your Savings – Claim Now!" to highlight the benefit.
- Use a call to action (CTA) such as "Try Risk-Free for 30 Days!" to remind them of your guarantee.
- Saying "Yes, I Want to Boost My Business!" in the first person establishes rapport.
- Say "Join 10,000 Satisfied Customers Today!" using Social Proof and your achievements as examples.

- Make it personal by advising them to "Begin Your Journey - Unlock Your Success!"

- To highlight the intended result and remind them of what they want, say something like, "Get the Results You Deserve – Order Today!"

- Make sure your CTA is consistent with the research you conducted in Step 2 regardless of what you decide to write.

- Your ultimate aim should be to get them excited about the outcomes they will experience rather than to get them to make a purchase.

Step 7: Editing for impact and clarity

After creating your captivating copy, it's time to hone your editing abilities. Your writing becomes exceptional through editing. Your primary priorities ought to be the following:

- Make sense: Make sure your message is understood clearly. Eliminate any technical words or jargon that could turn off your audience. Make difficult concepts understandable by simplifying them.
- Conciseness: Remove any excess. Remove any superfluous words, phrases, or paragraphs. Every word should be used to guide the reader toward the call to action.
- Make sure that the tone, style, and voice of your writing are all the same throughout. The reader's flow may be disturbed by inconsistencies.
- Grammar and Spelling: Misspellings and grammar mistakes damage your credibility. Carefully proofread (or make use of programs like Grammarly or the Hemmingway App).
- Formatting: To make your content readable (and skimmable), use headers,

bullet points, and brief paragraphs to break up the language.

Step 8: Evaluation and Revision

Iteration is key to great copywriting. It's time to test after you've edited. A/B testing is a useful tool if you want to rapidly evaluate what is (and isn't) working. Examine your copy's components (headlines, calls to action, and even the structure) rather than focusing on a single test. Monitor the effects of these adjustments on your conversion rates.

Writing persuasive copy is both an art and a science in the field of copywriting. Understanding your audience is key to effective copywriting. Highly effective copy uses tried-and-true methods to nudge readers in the direction of action.

www.ingramcontent.com/pod-product-compliance
Lightning Source LLC
Chambersburg PA
CBHW062342290526
45794CB00005B/2085